Handy Montana Genealogy Handbook

I0412034

Gary L. Morris

©2015 Gary L. Morris

ISBN-13: 978-1507837733

ISBN-10: 1507837739

Table of Contents

Notes

Genealogical Research in Montana

There are many genealogical records and resources available for tracing your family history in Montana. Because there are so many records held at many different locations, tracking down the records for your ancestor can be an ominous task. Don't worry though, we know just where they are, and we'll show you which records you'll need, while helping you to understand:

1. What they are
2. Where to find them
3. How to use them

These records can be found both online and off, so we'll introduce you to online websites, indexes and databases, as well as brick-and-mortar repositories and other institutions that will help with your research in Montana. So that you will have a more comprehensive understanding of these records, we have provided a brief history of the "Treasure State" to illustrate what type of records may have been generated during specific time periods. That information will assist you in pinpointing times and locations on which to focus the search for your Montana ancestors and their records.

A Brief History of Montana

The area now known as Montana was first inhabited by Native American tribes such as the Crows, Cheyenne, and Blackfeet. The first Europeans to enter the region were those of the Lewis and Clark Expedition of 1804-1806. Trappers and traders arrived soon after bringing alcohol, disease, and a new economic system to the natives. By the 1840's the population of beaver had disintegrated to such a level that it brought an end to the trapping industry. Most of Montana was included in the Louisiana Purchase of 1803.

The trappers who had come to Montana were soon followed by Catholic missionaries who established what is believed to be the first permanent settlement in Montana - Saint Mary's Mission in the Bitterroot Valley. The missionaries introduced agriculture to the region and constructed a sawmill, but Montana's economy really took off with the discovery of gold in the 1860's. Many prospectors flocked to the area, the rapid influx of people leading to boomtowns that shot up and declined just as quickly when gold deposits were exhausted.

Montana became a territory in 1864, and as the population of white settlers increased, so did the resentment of the native populace. Angry at the loss of their lands and traditional ways, the Native tribes went to war against the invaders. Some of the most famous battles between Native Americans and the U.S. Army took place in Montana, notably the Battle of Little Big Horn where General Custer and his troops were slain in 1876 and the Battle of Big Hole Basin in 1877 when Chief Joseph and the Nez Perce were victorious over U.S. troops.

The strength of the United States Army prevailed in the end however, and as the Indian resistance was ended, cattle ranches began to flourish and new mining communities emerged. Open range cattle ranching flourished across Montana's open plains, and the town of Butte became famous when copper and silver were discovered near there. Railroads crossed Montana by the 1880,s and the territory was made a state in 1889.

Important Dates in Montana History

1803– Part of Louisiana Purchase

1812 – Part of Missouri Territory

1846 – Northwestern Montana part of Oregon Territory

1853 – Northwestern Montana part of Washington Territory

1854 – Montana made part of Nebraska Territory

1861 – Becomes part of Dakota Territory

1863 – Northwestern Montana part of Idaho Territory

1864 – Montana made a separate territory

1876– Battle of Little Bighorn

1877 – Battle of Big Hole Basin

1889 – Statehood

Famous Battles Fought in Montana

Montana has had a relatively quiet military history, but two famous battles between Native American tribes and U.S. troops were fought in the state - the **Battle of Little Bighorn** in 1876, and the **Battle of Big Hole Basin** in 1877.

These battle accounts that exist can be very effective in uncovering the military records of your ancestor. They can tell you what regiments fought in which battles, and often include the names and ranks of many officers and enlisted men.

Battle of Little Bighorn:
http://www.eyewitnesstohistory.com/custer.htm

Battle of Big Hole Basin:
http://www.friendsnezpercebattlefields.org/battle-of-big-hole.htm

Common Montana Genealogical Issues and Resources to Overcome Them

Boundary Changes: Boundary changes are a common obstacle when researching Montana ancestors. You could be searching for an ancestor's record in one county when in fact it is stored in a different one due to historical county boundary changes.

The **Atlas of Historical County Boundaries** can help you to overcome that problem. It provides a chronological listing of every boundary change that has occurred in the history of Montana.

Atlas of Historical County Boundaries:
http://publications.newberry.org/ahcbp/documents/MT_Consolidated _Chronology.htm#Consolidated_Chronology

Name Changes: Surname changes, variations, and misspellings can complicate genealogical research. It is important to check all spelling variations. Soundex, a program that indexes names by sound, is a useful first step, but you can't rely on it completely as some name variations result in different Soundex codes. The surnames could be different, but the first name may be different too. You can also find records filed under initials, middle names, and nicknames as well, so you will need to **get creative with surname variations** and spellings in order to cover all the possibilities. For help with surname variations read our instructional article on **How to Use Soundex**.

get creative with surname variations:
http://obituarieshelp.org/blog/?p=634

How to Use Soundex: http://obituarieshelp.org/blog/?p=505

Montana Genealogical Organizations and Archives

Genealogical resources include not only records, but the organizations that house them, or can direct you to them. These institutions include: *Archives, Libraries, Genealogical Societies, Family History Centers, Universities, Churches, and Museums.*

Following are links to their websites, their physical addresses, and a summary of the records you can find there.

Archives and Libraries

Montana Historical Society (State Archives) - marriage records and naturalization records from the District Court Clerk's office, school census records, oral histories, manuscripts, city and county directories, newspapers and periodicals

P.O. Box 210201
225 North Roberts Street
Helena, MT 59620-1201
Telephone: 406-444-2694
Fax: 406-444-2696
Email: mhslibrary@mt.gov

Montana Historical Society:
http://www.montanahistoricalsociety.org/research/library/archcoll.asp

National Archives Rocky Mountain Region (Denver) – mining records, Native American records, naturalization records

17101 Huron Street
Broomfield, CO 80023
Telephone: 303-604-4740
Fax: 303-407-5707

National Archives Rocky Mountain Region (Denver):
http://www.archives.gov/denver/holdings/

University of Montana – variety of genealogical resources including; historical newspapers, African American studies, Native American studies, women's studies, local histories, historical maps

Mansfield Library
32 Campus Drive
Missoula, MT 59812-9936
Telephone: 406-243-6866
Fax: 406-243-4067

University of Montana: http://www.lib.umt.edu/

Montana State University – Native American records, historical journals, historical maps, research resources

Renne Library
P.O. Box 173320
Bozeman, MT 59717-3320
Telephone: 406-994-3119
Fax: 406-994-2851

Montana State University: http://www.lib.montana.edu/

Montana Genealogical and Historical Societies

Genealogical and historical societies have access to extensive catalogues of genealogical data. They are also able to offer expert guidance for genealogical researchers. Many members are professional genealogists who are most willing to share their expertise in finding ancestors.

Montana State Genealogical Society – genealogical research resources including local histories, cemetery records, church records, military records, city directories, land records, marriage records, and more

P.O. Box 5313
120 South Last Chance Gulch
Helena, MT 59604
Telephone 406-447-1690 Ext9

Montana State Genealogical Society: http://montanamsgs.org/

The Genealogy Forum website has an extensive listing of **Montana County Genealogical Societies**

Montana County Genealogical Societies:
http://www.genealogyforum.rootsweb.com/gfaol/resource/MT/HS.ht
m

Montana Mailing Lists

Mailing lists are internet based facilities that use email to distribute a single message to all who subscribe to it. When information on a particular surname, new records, or any other important genealogy information related to the mailing list topic becomes available, the subscribers are alerted to it. Joining a mailing list is an excellent way to stay up to date on Montana genealogy research topics. Rootsweb have an extensive listing of **Montana Mailing Lists** on a variety of topics.

Montana Mailing Lists:
http://lists.rootsweb.ancestry.com/index/usa/MT/misc.html

Montana Message Boards

A message board is another internet based facility where people can post questions about a specific genealogy topic and have it answered by other genealogists. If you have questions about a surname, record type, or research topic, you can post your question and other researchers and genealogists will help you with the answer. Be sure to check back regularly, as the answers are not emailed to you. The Montana message boards at **Rootsweb** are completely free to use.

Montana Genealogy Forum:
http://boards.rootsweb.com/localities.northam.usa.states/mb.ashx

Montana Newspapers and Periodicals

Many genealogy periodicals and historical newspapers contain reprinted copies of family genealogies, transcripts of family Bible records, information about local records and archives, census indexes, church records, queries, land records, obituaries, court records, cemetery records, and wills. The following sites have historical Montana newspapers and periodicals that you can search online or on-site.

Montana Historical Society (State Archives) - 95% of the papers ever published in Montana in 2,000 bound volumes and 17,000 reels of microfilm.

P.O. Box 210201
225 North Roberts Street
Helena, MT 59620-1201
Telephone: 406-444-2694
Fax: 406-444-2696
Email: mhslibrary@mt.gov

Montana Historical Society:
http://www.montanahistoricalsociety.org/research/library/archcoll.asp

GenealogyBank.com – free searchable database of Montana newspaper archives, 1866–1922

GenealogyBank.com:
http://www.genealogybank.com/gbnk/newspapers/explore/USA/Montana/

Library of Congress Digital Newspaper Directory – free searchable database of historical U.S. newspapers dating from 1690-present

Library of Congress Digital Newspaper Directory:
http://chroniclingamerica.loc.gov/search/titles/

The Online Books Page – links to historical Montana books and periodicals available for viewing online, dating from mid-16th century

The Online Books Page:
http://onlinebooks.library.upenn.edu/webbin/book//browse?type=lcsubc&key=Montana%20--%20History%20--%20Periodicals

NewspaperArchive.com – largest online database of historical newspapers in the world.

NewspaperArchive.com: http://newspaperarchive.com/

Historical Montana Maps and Gazetteers

Maps are an integral part of genealogical research. They help us to locate landmarks, towns, cities, parishes, states, provinces, waterways and roads and streets. They also help us to determine when and where boundary changes might have taken place, and give us a visualization of the area we're researching in.

For locating place names, a gazetteer is the best possible resource for any genealogist. Gazetteers are also sometimes called "place name dictionaries", and can help you to locate the area in which you need to conduct research. Below are links to the maps and gazetteers for research in Montana.

Peabody GNIS Service – Montana:
http://peabody.research.yale.edu/cgi-bin/Query.GNIS?ST=Montana&SU=1

Color Landform Atlas – Montana:
http://fermi.jhuapl.edu/states/mt_0.html

1985 U.S. Atlas: http://www.livgenmi.com/1895/MT/

Montana Hometown Locator:
http://montana.hometownlocator.com/

Montana City Directories

.

City directories are similar to telephone directories in that they list the residents of a particular area. The difference though is what is important to genealogists, and that is they pre-date telephone directories. You can find an ancestor's information such as their street address, place of employment, occupation, or the name of their spouse. A one-stop-shop for finding city directories in Montana is the **Montana Online Historical Directories** which contains a listing of every available online historical directory related to Montana.

Montana Online Historical Directories:
https://sites.google.com/site/onlinedirectorysite/Home/usa/mt

Montana State Genealogical Society – City directories for the major towns in Montana, plus many directories often including the smaller surrounding towns and farmers/ranchers in nearby counties, especially for the 1900-1920 period

P.O. Box 5313
120 South Last Chance Gulch
Helena, MT 59604
Telephone 406-447-1690 Ext9

Montana State Genealogical Society:
http://montanahistorywiki.pbworks.com

Montana Genealogical Records

<u>Birth, Death, Marriage and Divorce Records</u> – Also known as vital records, birth, death, and marriage certificates are the most basic, yet most important records attached to your ancestor. The reason for their importance is that they not only place your ancestor in a specific place at a definite time, but potentially connect the individual to other relatives. Below is a list of repositories and websites where you can find Montana vital records.

Statewide registration of births and deaths was not required until 1907, although a few Montana counties kept birth and death records prior to 1895. Those records are kept by the **Clerks of the County Court.**

Clerks of the County Court:
http://courts.mt.gov/locator/default.mcpx

Montana Department of Public Health and Human Services – birth and death certificates 1907 to present, marriages 1943 to present, divorces 1954 to present

Office of Vital Statistics
111 N Sanders, Room 209
Helena, MT 59604
Telephone: 1-888-877-1946
Email: HHSVitalRecords@mt.gov

Montana Department of Public Health and Human Services:
https://dphhs.mt.gov/certificates/ordercertificates.shtml

Montana State Genealogical Society – Death indexes, 1800-1919, 1920-1929, 1930-1939, 1940-1949 and 1950-1953

P.O. Box 5313
120 South Last Chance Gulch
Helena, MT 59604
Telephone 406-447-1690 Ext9

Montana State Genealogical Society:
http://www.rootsweb.ancestry.com/~mtmsgs/death_records.htm

Family Search has the following indexes which can be searched online for free:

Montana, County Births and Deaths, 1840-2004:
https://familysearch.org/search/collection/1930397

Montana, County Marriages, 1865-1950:
https://familysearch.org/search/collection/1609797

Montana, Death Index, 1860-2007:
https://familysearch.org/search/collection/1941331

Montana, Marriages, 1889-1947:
https://familysearch.org/search/collection/1675397

Census Reports

Census records are among the most important genealogical documents for placing your ancestor in a particular place at a specific time. Like BDM records, they can also lead you to other ancestors, particularly those who were living under the authority of the head of household.

Federal census records for Montana exist from 1860–1940 and can be found at:

National Archives – Federal census Schedules for all states, 1790-1940

8601 Adelphi Road
College Park, MD 20740-6001
Tel: 1-866-272-6272

National Archives: http://www.archives.gov/research/census/

Free Census Project: http://usgwcensus.org/cenfiles/mt.htm

Access Genealogy – Montana county census records from 1870-1930

Access Genealogy:
http://www.accessgenealogy.com/census/montana-census-records.htm

African American Census Schedules Online – slave schedules, mortality schedules, slave-owners census

African American Census Schedules Online:
http://www.afrigeneas.com/aacensus/

Montana Church Records

Church and synagogue records are a valuable resource, especially for baptisms, marriages, and burials that took place before 1900. You will need to at least have an idea of your ancestor's religious denomination, and in most cases you will have to visit a brick and mortar establishment to view them.

Most church records are kept by the individual church, although in some denominations, records are placed in a regional archive or maintained at the diocesan level. Local Historical Societies are sometimes the repository for the state's older church records. Below are links archives that maintain church records, as well as a few databases that can be viewed online.

The **Family History Library** contains many church records from a variety of denominations on microfilm.

Family History Library:
http://familysearch.org/learn/wiki/en/Family_History_Library

Montana State Genealogical Society – variety Catholic Church, Vicariate Apostolic of Nebraska, Montana Missions--Indexed record book, 1866-1882, of baptisms, marriages, births, deaths, confirmation in Helena, Hellgate Missoula, and Frenchtown, Catholic Church, Vicariate Apostolic of Nebraska, Montana Missions--Indexed Book of Functions, 1877-1902, for the Missoula Mission, Episcopal Church (Virginia City)--Baptisms, marriages, burials, church membership, 1867-1958, Evangelical Lutheran Church (Helena)--Baptisms, marriages, burials, 1884-1950; also included Butte, Deer Lodge, and Bozeman

P.O. Box 5313
120 South Last Chance Gulch
Helena, MT 59604
Telephone 406-447-1690 Ext9

Montana State Genealogical Society link to:
http://montanahistorywiki.pbworks.com

Central Repositories for Denominational Records

Church of Jesus Christ of Latter-day Saints (Mormons)

Early Mormon Church records for Montana can be found on film located at the LDS Family History Library in Salt Lake City and can be searched via the **Family History Library Catalog**

Family History Library Catalog:
https://familysearch.org/eng/Library/FHLC/frameset_fhlc.asp

Methodist

Montana Methodist Historical Society

Paul M. Adams Memorial Library
Rocky Mountain College
1511 Poly Drive
Billings, MT 59102
Phone: 406-657-1000 or 1-800-877-6259
Fax: 406-259-9751

Paul M. Adams Memorial Library:
http://www.rocky.edu/academics/library/Archives.php

Presbyterian

Presbyterian Historical Society

United Presbyterian Church in the United States
425 Lombard Street
Philadelphia, PA 19147-1516
Phone: 215-627-1852
Fax: 215-627-0509
Email: Refdesk@history.pcusa.org

Presbyterian Historical Society: http://www.history.pcusa.org/

<u>Roman Catholic</u>

Diocese of Great Falls—Billings
121 23rd Street South
P.O. Box 1399
Great Falls, MT 59403-1399
Phone: 406-727-6683
Fax: 406-454-3480

Diocese of Great Falls—Billings: http://diocesegfb.org/

Diocese of Helena Archive
515 North Ewing
P.O. Box 1729
Helena, MT 59624-1729
Phone: 406-442-5820

Diocese of Helena Archive:
http://www.diocesehelena.org/offices/archives/accessing-archives.html#geneological

Montana Military Records

More than 40 million Americans have participated in some time of war service since America was colonized. The chance of finding your ancestor amongst those records is exceptionally high. Military records can even reveal individuals who never actually served, such as those who registered for the two World Wars but were never called to duty.

Below are a number of links to websites and archives that contain Montana military records.

U.S. National Archives – Records of United States Army Continental Commands, 1821-1920 (contains records of a number of forts established throughout Montana and includes information and documents such as: registers, reports, and correspondence), WWI Draft registration cards, casualties lists, WWI and WWII service records, Korean War records, Vietnam War records, Civil War and Spanish-American War records, and casualties lists.

U.S. National Archives:
http://www.archives.gov/research/military/veterans/online.html

US Department of Veterans Affairs Nationwide Gravesite Locator – includes information on veterans and their family members buried in veterans and military cemeteries having a government grave marker.

US Department of Veterans Affairs Nationwide Gravesite Locator: **http://gravelocator.cem.va.gov/**

You may also find your ancestor's military records in the following databases:

United States General Index to Pension Files, 1861-1934:
https://familysearch.org/search/collection/1919699

United States Index to Service Records, War with Spain, 1898
link to: https://familysearch.org/search/collection/1919583

United States Index to Indian Wars Pension Files, 1892-1926 –
military pension records of soldiers who fought in the Indian Wars
between 1817 and 1898

United States Index to Indian Wars Pension Files, 1892-1926:
https://familysearch.org/search/collection/1979427

United States Registers of Enlistments in the U.S. Army, 1798-1914 - index of men who enlisted in the United States Army, 1798-1914.

United States Registers of Enlistments in the U.S. Army, 1798-1914: https://familysearch.org/search/collection/1880762

United States Mexican War Pension Index, 1887-1926 - index to
Mexican War pension files for service between 1846 and 1848

United States Mexican War Pension Index, 1887-1926:
https://familysearch.org/search/collection/1979390

Civil War Soldiers Service Records - Service records for both
Union and Confederate soldiers indexed by soldier's name, rank, and
unit.

Civil War Soldier Service Records:
http://go.fold3.com/civilwar_records/

Montana Cemetery Records

As convenient as it is to search cemetery records online, keep in mind that there are a few disadvantages over visiting a cemetery in person. They are:

- Tombstone information is not always accurately transcribed
- The arrangement of the graves in a cemetery can be crucial as family members are often buried next to each other or in the same grave. This arrangement is not always preserved in the alphabetical indexes that are found online.

With that information in mind, the following websites have databases that can be searched online for Montana Cemetery records.

Montana State Genealogical Society – variety of cemetery and funeral home records dating from 1865-1971

P.O. Box 5313
120 South Last Chance Gulch
Helena, MT 59604
Telephone 406-447-1690 Ext9

Montana State Genealogical Society link to:
http://montanahistorywiki.pbworks.com

Montana Tombstone Transcription Project - death and burial records

Montana Tombstone Transcription Project:
http://www.usgwtombstones.org/montana/montana.html

African American Cemeteries Online – African American, slave, and Native American cemetery records

African American Cemeteries Online:
http://africanamericancemeteries.com/

Access Genealogy – huge database of Montana cemetery record transcriptions

Access Genealogy:
http://www.accessgenealogy.com/cemetery/montana-cemetery-records.htm

Find a Grave – over 100 million grave records can be searched on this site. Search can be conducted by name, location, or cemetery name.

Find a Grave: http://www.findagrave.com/

Interment.net - A free online database containing approximately 4 million cemetery records from around the world.

Interment.net: http://www.interment.net/

Billion Graves – as the name implies, you can search a billion records including headstone photos, transcriptions, cemetery records, and grave locations.

Billion Graves:
http://billiongraves.com/pages/search/index.php#cemetery

Montana Obituaries

Obituaries can reveal a wealth about our ancestor and other relatives. You can search our **Montana Newspaper Obituaries Listings** from hundreds of Montana newspapers online for free.

Montana Newspaper Obituaries Listings:
http://obituarieshelp.org/montana_newspaper_obituaries.html

Montana Wills and Probate Records

The documents found in a probate packet may include a complete inventory of a person's estate, newspaper entries, witness testimony, a copy of a will, list of debtors and creditors, names of executors or trustees, names of heirs. They can not only tell you about the ancestor you're currently researching, but lead to other ancestors.

Montana probate records have are kept by the **Clerks of the County Court**.

Clerks of the County Court:
http://courts.mt.gov/locator/default.mcpx

Family Search has the following indexes that can be searched online for free:

Montana, Beaverhead County Records, 1862-2009:
https://familysearch.org/search/collection/2075129

Montana, Big Horn, County Records, 1884-2011:
https://familysearch.org/search/collection/2117001

Montana, Cascade County Records, 1880-2009:
https://familysearch.org/search/collection/1926700

Montana, Chouteau County Records, 1876-2011:
https://familysearch.org/search/collection/2028318

Montana, Flathead County Records, 1871-1981:
https://familysearch.org/search/collection/1387035

Montana, Granite County Records, 1865-2009:
https://familysearch.org/search/collection/2029197

Montana, Judith Basin County Records, 1887-2012:
https://familysearch.org/search/collection/2110919

Montana, Lake County Records, 1857-2010:
https://familysearch.org/search/collection/1986787

Montana, Rosebud County Records:
https://familysearch.org/search/collection/1908714

Montana, Sanders County Records, 1866-2010:
https://familysearch.org/search/collection/2109937

Montana, Sweet Grass County Records, 1887-2011:
https://familysearch.org/search/collection/2036960

Montana, Yellowstone County Records, 1881-2011:
https://familysearch.org/search/collection/2013531

Montana Immigration and Naturalization Records

The naturalization process generated many types of records, including petitions, declarations of intention, and oaths of allegiance. These records can provide family historians with information such as a person's birth date and place of birth, immigration year, marital status, spouse information, occupation, witnesses' names and addresses, and more.

National Archives Rocky Mountain Region (Denver) – naturalization documents, declarations and petitions from the Federal courts of the Mountain West states

17101 Huron Street
Broomfield, CO 80023
Telephone: 303-604-4740
Fax: 303-407-5707

National Archives Rocky Mountain Region (Denver): http://www.archives.gov/denver/holdings/

U.S. National Archives – Immigration and Naturalization records, 1787-1993

U.S. National Archives: http://www.archives.gov/research/guide-fed-records/groups/085.html

Montana Native American Records

Montana State University – Fort Belknap Indian Reservation Records, 1874-1977, Indian Claims Commission Research Papers, 1855-1979, Crow Indian Agency Fraud Hearings Collection, 1876-1877, Biographical materials, publications, correspondence, research files, and photographs for Blackfeet, Blood, Kutenai, Cheyenne, Shoshoni and Arapaho Indians

Renne Library
P.O. Box 173320
Bozeman, MT 59717-3320
Telephone: 406-994-3119
Fax: 406-994-2851

Montana State University: http://www.lib.montana.edu/

Access Genealogy – Montana Native American census records, tribal histories, and much more

Access Genealogy:
http://www.accessgenealogy.com/native/montana-indian-tribes.htm

U.S. National Archives - information on American Indians who maintained their ties to Federally-recognized Tribes (1830-1970).

U.S. National Archives: http://www.archives.gov/research/native-americans/

Records of the Bureau of Indian Affairs (BIA):
http://www.archives.gov/research/guide-fed-records/groups/075.html

American Indians Records Repository - records dating from the 1700s including trust, education and other historic Indian Affairs records

American Indian Records Repository
Meritex Enterprises
17501 West 98th Street
Lenexa, KS 66219
Phone: 913-888-0601

American Indians Records Repository:
http://www.doi.gov/ost/records_mgmt/american-indian-records-repository.cfm

Missing Matriarchs – Resources for Researching Female Montana Ancestors

Looking for female ancestors requires an adjustment of how we view traditional records sources. A woman's identity was often under that of her husband, and often individual records for them can be difficult to locate. The following resources are effective in locating female ancestors in Montana where traditional records may not reveal them.

<u>Bibliographies</u>

1. *Montana: A History of Two centuries,* Michael P. Malone (University of Washington Press, 1991)
2. *No Step Backward: Women and Family on the Rocky Mountain Mining Frontiers, Helena, Montana,* Paula Petrick (Montana Historical Society Press, 1987)
3. *Girl From the Gulches,* Ellen Baumier (Montana Historical Society Press, 2012)
4. *More Than Petticoats: Montana's Remarkable Women,* Gayle C. Shirley (Twodot, 1995)

Selected Resources for Montana Women's History

Montana Women's History Project
Mansfield Library
University of Montana
2626 Garland
Missoula, MT 59812

Montana Historical Society
P.O. Box 210201
225 North Roberts Street
Helena, MT 59620-1201
Telephone: 406-444-2694
Fax: 406-444-2696
Email: mhslibrary@mt.gov

Common Montana Surnames

The following surnames are among the most common in Montana and are also being currently researched by other genealogists. If you find your surname here, there is a chance that some research has already been performed on your ancestor.

Beaverhead, Big Horn, Blaine, Broadwater, Carbon, Carter, Cascade, Chouteau, Custer, Daniels, Dawson, DeerLodge, Fallon, Fergus, Flathead, Gallatin, Garfield, Glacie, GoldenValley, Granite, Hill, Jefferson, Lake, Lewis, Liberty, Lincoln, Madison, McCone, Meagher, Mineral, Missoula, Musselshell, Park, Petroleum, Phillips, Pondera, Powder River, Powell, Prairie, Ravalli, Richland, Roosevelt, Rosebud, Sanders, Sheridan, Silver Bow, Stillwater, Sweet Grass, Teton, Toole, Treasure, Valley, Wheatland, Wibaux, Yellowstone

About the Author

Gary L. Morris worked from 2009 to 2014 as a professional researcher for a major player in the genealogy field. After tracing his family lineage back to 1683, he found that genealogy could be an expensive undertaking. As such, has decided to publish these helpful guides to share the valuable free information he has discovered during his career to help others trace their family lineages as inexpensively as possible. An avid genealogist himself, he hopes you will find this guide factual, thorough, helpful, and most of all, effective in helping you to find your family members.

Notes

Notes

Native Americans in Census Records (US National Archives):
http://www.archives.gov/research/census/native-americans/

www.ingramcontent.com/pod-product-compliance
Lightning Source LLC
Chambersburg PA
CBHW070517290526
45790CB00003B/1246